Surviving Tsunamis

Kevin Cunningham

www.raintreepublishers.co.uk
Visit our website to find out more information about Raintree books.

To order:
☎ Phone 0845 6044371
🖷 Fax +44 (0) 1865 312263
🖳 Email myorders@raintreepublishers.co.uk

Customers from outside the UK please telephone +44 1865 312262

Raintree is an imprint of **Capstone Global Library Limited**, a company incorporated in England and Wales having its registered office at 7 Pilgrim Street, London, EC4V 6LB – Registered company number: 6695582

Text © Capstone Global Library Limited 2011
First published in hardback in 2011
First published in paperback in 2012
The moral rights of the proprietor have been asserted.

Edited by Louise Galpine and Laura Knowles
Designed by Victoria Allen
Original illustrations © Capstone Global Library Limited 2011
Illustrated by HLSTUDIOS
Picture research by Ruth Blair
Originated by Capstone Global Library Limited
Printed and bound in China by CTPS

ISBN 978 1 406 22218 0 (hardback)
15 14 13 12 11
10 9 8 7 6 5 4 3 2 1

ISBN 978 1 406 22225 8 (paperback)
16 15 14 13 12
10 9 8 7 6 5 4 3 2 1

British Library Cataloguing in Publication Data
Cunningham, Kevin
Surviving tsunamis. -- (Children's true stories. Natural disasters)
363.3'494-dc22
A full catalogue record for this book is available from the British Library.

Acknowledgements
We would like to thank the following for permission to reproduce photographs: Corbis pp. **8** (© Bettmann), **19** (© Bettmann), **22** (© Benjamin Lowy), **23** (© Jeremy Horner), **27** (© Manjunath Kiran/EPA); Getty Images p. **18** (TIME & LIFE Images); © Mila Zinkova p. **15**; NOAA pp. **4** (EDIS), **11** (Harry A Simms, Sr), **12** (NGDC Natural Hazards Photo Archive), **13** (NGDC Natural Hazards Photo Archive), **14**, **17** (U.S. Geological Survey); PA Photos p. **21** (Edmond Terakopian/PA Archive); The Rooms Provisional Archives Division pp. **7** (S. H. Parsons & Sons), **9** (Miller); © TVE Asia Pacific p. **25**.

Cover photograph of people fleeing as a tsunami wave comes crashing ashore at Koh Raya, part of Thailand's territory in the Andaman islands and only some 23 kilometers from Phuket island, southern Thailand, 26 December 2004, reproduced with permission of Getty Images/John Russell/AFP.

Quotations on pages 7 and 9 are from Gary Cranford, *Not Too Long Ago: Seniors Tell Their Stories*, St. Johns, Newfoundland: The Seniors Resource Centre, 1999. Quotation on page 11 is from Ned Rozell, "1946 tsunami survivor shares her story", Alaska Report, May 13, 2009, www.alaskareport.com. Quotation on page 13 is from the *Honolulu Star Bulletin*, April 5, 1946, as in Sarah Davidson, "Mystery of Deadly 1946 Tsunami Deepens", *LiveScience*, December 6, 2004, www.livescience.com. Quotations on pages 17 is from Dennis M. Powers, *The Raging Sea: The Powerful Account of the Worst Tsunami in U.S. History*, Citadel Press, 2005. Quotations on pages 20 and 21 are from "Award for tsunami warning pupil", BBC News, September 9, 2005, news.bbc.co.uk. Quotation on page 23 is from Jessica Horing, "From Fear to Survival: Knowledge is Key", ABC News, January 22, 2009, abcnews.go.com. Heshani Madushika Hewavitharana's story on page 25 is from Children of Tsunami, www.childrenoftsunami.info.

We would like to thank Daniel Block for his invaluable help in the preparation of this book.

Every effort has been made to contact copyright holders of material reproduced in this book. Any omissions will be rectified in subsequent printings if notice is given to the publisher.

Disclaimer
All the internet addresses (URLs) given in this book were valid at the time of going to press. However, due to the dynamic nature of the internet, some addresses may have changed, or sites may have changed or ceased to exist since publication. While the author and publisher regret any inconvenience this may cause readers, no responsibility for any such changes can be accepted by either the author or the publisher.

Contents

DAILY LIFE

Read here to learn about what life was like for the children in these stories, and the impact the disaster had at home and school.

NUMBER CRUNCHING

Find out here the details about natural disasters and the damage they cause.

Survivors' lives

Read these boxes to find out what happened to the children in this book when they grew up.

HELPING HAND

Find out how people and organizations have helped to save lives.

On the scene

Read eyewitness accounts of the natural disasters in the survivors' own words.

Some words are printed in bold, **like this**. You can find out what they mean by looking in the glossary on page 30.

Introduction

The word *tsunami* means "harbour wave" in Japanese. A tsunami happens when an underwater earthquake, volcano, or avalanche shakes up the ocean. But a tsunami is not a single wave. It is a number of waves that may be anywhere from five minutes to an hour apart. The waves can travel at up to 950 kilometres per hour (590 miles per hour).

A tsunami strikes Hilo, Hawaii, in 1946. The man on the left was one of the victims.

Oddly enough, in deep water a tsunami looks like nothing more than a small ripple. As it passes through shallow water, however, it grows into a large wave. The wall of water crashes into the shore with tremendous force. In moments, flat areas along the shore are flooded. Buildings may break apart. People must run for higher ground or risk being swept away.

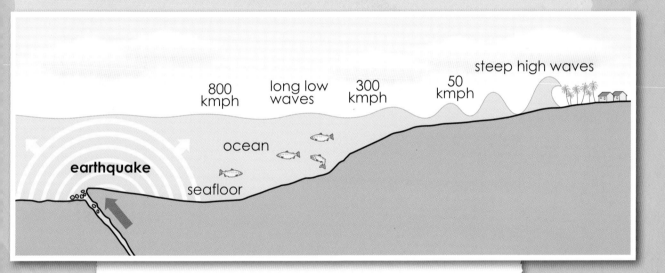

This diagram shows how the height of a tsunami grows as it reaches the shallow water near the shore.

HELPING HAND

The following are the tsunami survival rules from the United States Geological Survey:

- Take tsunami warnings seriously
- If at school, listen to teachers about what to do
- Get away from the water and move to higher ground
- Once safe, stay where you are. Several tsunami waves may hit.
- Abandon belongings. Save your life, not your things.

Kelly's Cove, Newfoundland: 1929

Kelly's Cove was a small village on the coast of the Atlantic Ocean. Just after 5.00 p.m. on 18 November 1929, people there felt a **tremor**. Nobody realized that an earthquake had torn up the sea floor about 250 kilometres (150 miles) out to sea. At around 7.30 p.m., people near the shore saw the water rush out of the bay, away from land.

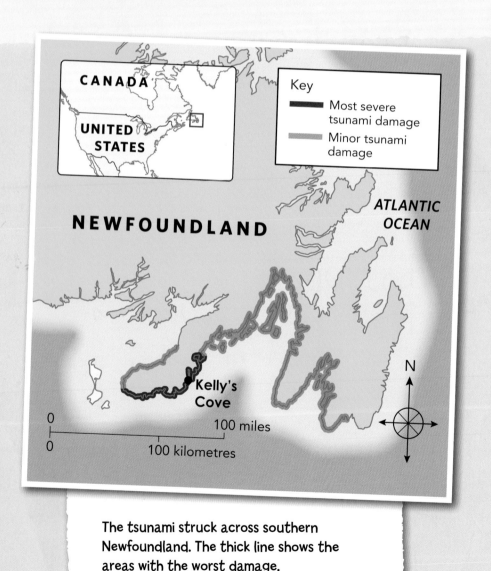

The tsunami struck across southern Newfoundland. The thick line shows the areas with the worst damage.

Pearl's story

Pearl Brushett, aged five, lay in bed with her sister Lillian. Their father was away cutting wood. Their mother Carrie and older sister Lottie sat downstairs. Without warning, a tsunami roared into Kelly's Cove. Pearl's mother woke up the girls. A moment later Pearl looked out of the window to see broken boats everywhere. Then she noticed her house had moved. The water had washed it out to sea with the Brushett family inside.

A tsunami can destroy buildings.

On the scene

Marion Kelly was doing her homework as the tsunami approached. "Well, you could hear the sea coming in," she later told the Seniors Resource Centre in St. John's, Newfoundland. "It was roaring. Of course we all ran out in the yard to see what was going on. The sea was just like a mountain coming, but slowly."

The escape

A second wave carried the Brushett's house back to shore. When it settled, two neighbours rushed to help. Pearl's mother cut her wrist as she smashed a large downstairs window to escape. The Brushetts hurried out through the window. Pearl's sister Lottie also cut herself on the glass. The neighbours bandaged them up. As soon as that was done, everyone ran to a nearby hill. They waited there as another wave struck the town. Once again the house floated into the ocean. Luckily, it remained in one piece. In fact, the family's cat was still safe inside.

Houses in Kelly's Cove were tossed over by the tsunami's **surge**.

Back to shore

Pearl's father returned and had a boat tow the house back to shore. During the trip the cat jumped into the water and swam to dry land. Afterwards, the Brushetts turned the damp house into a place to store fish.

"I had nightmares for a long time after," Pearl said. "In my dream I was always going up a hill and the water was always a few feet behind me."

A boat tows a house back to land in Port au Bras, Newfoundland.

HELPING HAND

A parent's presence makes a big difference when disaster strikes. As Pearl Brushett said, "Mum was there, so naturally we figured Mum was going to look after us."

Hilo, Hawaii: 1946

On 1 April 1946, a major earthquake shook the seabed off Alaska's coast. In just under five hours, a tsunami reached Hilo, Hawaii.

Jeanne's story

That morning, 6-year-old Jeanne Branch and her younger brother David woke up at their grandparents' house near the ocean. The house was in a nice neighbourhood. Coconut trees towered over the gardens. Sugar cane grew near by.

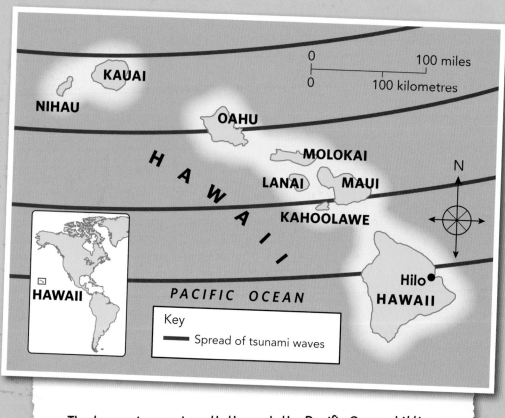

The tsunami spread south through the Pacific Ocean, hitting the coast of Hawaii.

Disaster approaches

A blare of car horns interrupted Jeanne as she got ready for school. Curious, she went outside. David followed. To their surprise, **debris** was scattered all over the garden. The horns, Jeanne learned later, came from cars in a traffic jam, where a tsunami had washed away the road.

Jeanne wanted to stay outside to see what would happen next. But when red ants swarmed over David's feet he made her take him back into the house. Once indoors, the children returned upstairs to the kitchen. A moment later, a second wave from the tsunami came ashore. It was far larger than the one that had damaged the road. Sometimes luck plays a role in surviving a tsunami. As Jeanne said, she and her brother "wouldn't have been here today if it hadn't been for those red ants".

Rod Mason, Jeanne's uncle, took this photograph of the tsunami hitting Hilo's shoreline.

Running for higher ground

Water surged through the ground floor of Jeanne's grandparents' house. When Jeanne looked outside, she saw water standing as high as her grandmother's washing line. Going upstairs had probably saved her and David's life.

Outside, a neighbour named Eddie called people together. He had a plan to get to higher ground. But trees and bushes as thick as jungle stood in the way. Eddie took the lead and chopped a path with a **machete**. Jeanne and others from the neighbourhood followed. The whole time the adults called for everyone to run. Another wave from the tsunami was nearing the shore.

Before the tsunami struck Hawaii, it hit the Alaska coast, which was near the earthquake zone. This photograph shows a **lighthouse** on Alaska's coast before the tsunami struck.

In the photograph below, the lighthouse is no longer there. The photo was taken after a wave 42 metres (137 feet) high destroyed the lighthouse and killed the 5 people inside.

On the scene

A newspaper from Hawaii's capital city, Honolulu, described how local resident Hilario Aquino became a hero. "Aquino said that when the waves hit the church, he was tossed out amidst the children. He swam about rescuing the children and lifting them up into the large trees of the church yard."

The power of the waves

Jeanne and David fled through the trees. On the other side they had to cross jagged, cooled **lava**. Jeanne was barefoot and cut her feet on the rocks. The group reached the high ground and waited. Below, another wave from the tsunami threw Jeanne's grandparents' house into the back garden. Her grandfather had stayed with the house. He got inside just in time and was not hurt. When the tsunami ended, Jeanne and the others went back to their neighbourhood. Waves had moved buildings from one side of the road to the other. On the way home, Jeanne saw one house lying upside-down.

Tsunami waves bent parking meters and ripped buildings apart.

IN MEMORY OF
THOSE WHO LOST THEIR LIVES IN THE TIDAL WAVE
APRIL 1, 1946

Sixteen students, five teachers, and three others died
when the tsunami struck Hilo's Laupahoehoe Park.
A **monument** to the victims stands in the park.

Jeanne's life now

The tsunami has had a big influence on Jeanne's life. At university
she wrote about tsunamis and also studied how to prepare for
and deal with disasters. From 2005–2008 she served as Hawaii's
earthquake and tsunami **programme planner**.

But the disaster also affected her in personal ways. She dreamt
about the tsunami for years. Then, in the early 1990s, she talked
about it in an interview. After that, the dreams stopped. She later
helped to found the Pacific Tsunami Museum in Hilo.

Crescent City, California, USA: 1964

The second-largest earthquake ever recorded struck Alaska on the evening of Friday 28 March 1964. Like a similar earthquake in 1946, it churned up tsunamis that swept south. The Alaskan coast and Canada's Vancouver Island suffered damage. Less destructive waves rolled into Japan, Mexico, and the Pacific Coast of South America. The greatest damage occurred, however, when the tsunami rushed on to the shore of Crescent City, California.

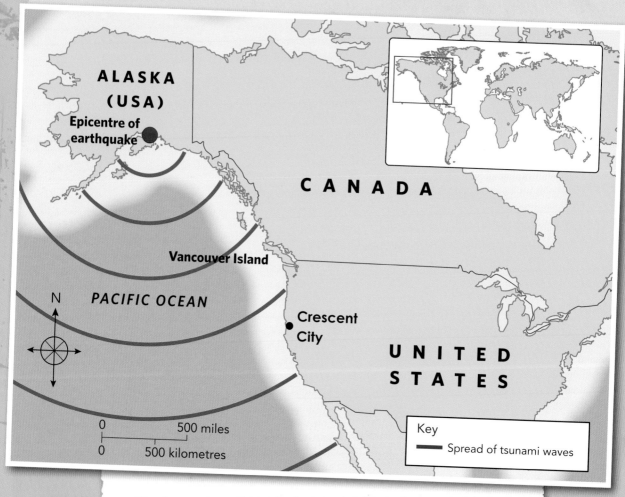

The tsunami crashed into Crescent City as it spread out from the earthquake's **epicentre** in Alaska.

Boys' story

School friends Rick Lillienthal, Rick Cardwell, and Floyd Stewart were sleeping in a tent near the shore. Outside the tent lay Feather, a cocker spaniel. Feather sensed the tsunami. The dog howled and barked at the boys, and finally licked their faces to wake them.

A roaring noise brought them out of the tent. A full moon lit the shore, and they saw the wave smash a small boat. The sea headed straight for their tent. They all took a deep breath as the water crashed into them.

In Whittier, Alaska, the tsunami drove a wooden plank through a car tyre.

On the scene

Crescent City lighthouse keeper Peggy Coons had a close-up view of the disaster. "When the tsunami assaulted the shore, it was like a violent explosion," she said. "Everywhere we looked, buildings, cars, timber, and boats shifted around like crazy."

Swept up by the tsunami

The boys could swim, but at first they had no chance against the **currents** in the moving water. Finally, they were able to get to the surface. The water carried them **inland**. Each boy grabbed debris to keep himself afloat. When the water calmed, they and Feather swam towards higher ground.

More than 1,000 cars were destroyed in Crescent City.

A second wave hit. Water again moved inland. By then however, the three boys had reached higher ground and could safely watch what was happening. The sea swept away again. Rick Lillienthal's house was near by. They arrived soon after with Feather alongside them. Later on, a newspaper story about them praised the dog for saving their lives. Others were not as lucky. Eleven people died in Crescent City. The 1964 tsunami is the deadliest ever to have struck the state of California.

The tsunami flooded the centre of Crescent City.

HELPING HAND

The morning after the tsunami, the Salvation Army and an American Legion Post were already handing out coffee and food. The American Red Cross, meanwhile, fed survivors and found shelter for those who had lost their homes. Over the following days, aid workers found people places to live, gave out money for food and clothing, and helped rebuild houses and businesses.

Phuket, Thailand: 2004

On 26 December 2004, 10-year-old Tilly Smith was on holiday with her family in Phuket, Thailand, when she saw something strange. "I noticed that when we went down to the sea, the sea was all frothy like on the top of a beer," she told a television station. "It was bubbling." Then the water rushed away from the shore.

About an hour and a half earlier, an earthquake had taken place near Indonesia. Tsunamis created by the earthquake were crossing the Indian Ocean in all directions. Waves had already smashed into Indonesia and Sri Lanka.

This map shows how the tsunami spread out from the earthquake epicentre, crashing into Phuket, and the coast of surrounding countries.

MYANMAR

N

THAILAND

ANDAMAN
SEA

Phuket

0 — 300 miles
0 — 300 kilometres

MALAYSIA

Epicentre of
earthquake

INDIAN OCEAN

INDONESIA

Key

— Spread of
tsunami waves

Land hit by
the tsunami

Tilly's story

Tilly knew about tsunamis. Just two weeks earlier, her geography teacher had shown her class a video of the 1946 Hawaii tsunami. Tilly told her parents that a bubbling sea and a quick retreat of water were signs that a tsunami was on its way. At first they didn't believe her. Finally she put her foot down. "I went, 'Right, I'm going to leave you, I know there is going to be a tsunami.'"

Off shore, boats began to bob up and down. A wave was growing as it reached shallow water. The tsunami bore down on Phuket's beach.

Tilly Smith's school lessons taught her to recognize the signs of a tsunami.

Tilly's warning gets through

Colin, Tilly's father, agreed to leave the beach with her. He was not convinced that Tilly was right. But he still told a security guard on the beach that, as strange as it sounded, Tilly was sure a tsunami was on the way. The security guard took Tilly seriously. He began to warn people on the beach. As tourists returned to the hotel, Colin called for his wife to come back.

Thousands of people died when the tsunami struck **Banda Aceh**, Indonesia, 20 minutes after the earthquake.

Wall of water

By then, a wall of water had appeared. Tilly's mother hurried towards them. She screamed for Colin to grab the kids. The Smiths dashed inside the hotel and headed upstairs.

Seconds later, the tsunami crashed over the beach. Water destroyed furniture, doors, and everything else in its way as it crashed into the hotel's ground floor. The Smiths stood on their balcony and watched in amazement.

This wave came ashore at Ao Nang, Thailand. It is very dangerous to stop and take photographs if a tsunami is heading towards you.

HELPING HAND

Author and disaster expert Amanda Ripley said, "This is a story that gives us a lot of hope, because if a 10-year-old girl can save people from a tsunami with basic information, then certainly we are all capable of that."

After the tsunami

Tilly had saved her family and about 100 people in the hotel. But over 230,000 people died in the many countries hit by the catastrophe. People often had no idea that a tsunami was coming. The Indian Ocean lacked a warning system. Millions of survivors had nowhere to go. The waves had destroyed their villages. They had also lost loved ones.

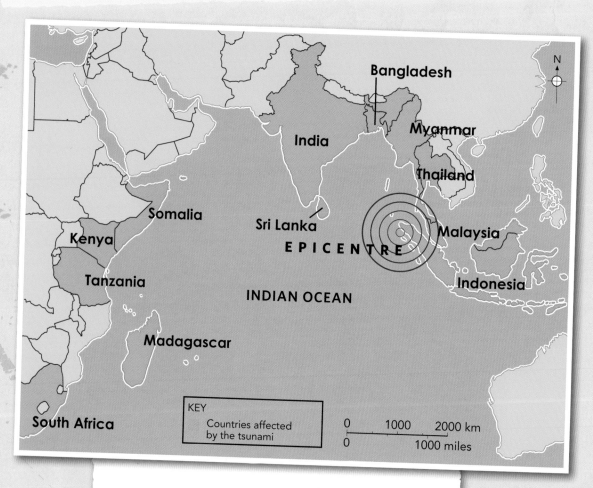

Tsunami waves created by the earthquake hit countries all around the Indian Ocean.

Heshani Madushika Hewavitharana, aged 13, lived in Suduwella on the coast of Sri Lanka. The tsunami wrecked everything her family owned. Her father even lost the boat he used to make a living. After the disaster, the family had to live in a single room at a friend's house. What happened to Heshani happened to many children.

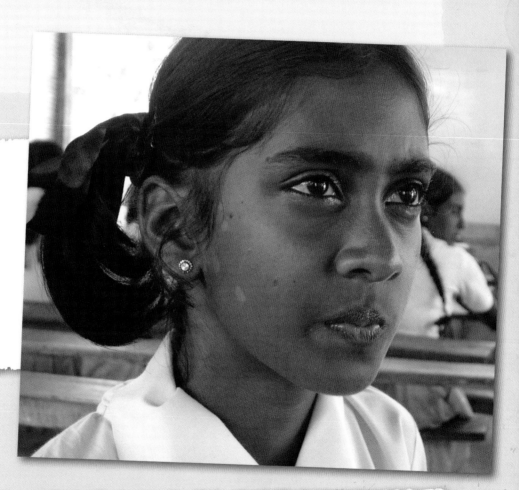

Even though life has been hard for Heshani and her family since the tsunami, Heshani has gone back to school and is glad to have survived.

DAILY LIFE

A **charity group** helped Heshani's family build a one-room house. It was so small, Heshani could not have her own room. It did not even have a kitchen. In September 2005, the charity group People in Peril gave Heshani's family a larger house. It was nearer to her school and away from the shore. The new, better house made daily life much easier for Heshani and her family.

Conclusion

The 2004 disaster changed the way people thought about tsunamis. The Indian Ocean clearly needed a tsunami warning system. Warnings, people realized, could have saved millions of lives. A **United Nations** agency led an effort to place machines that could measure earthquakes and send alarms. The new Indian Ocean tsunami warning system launched in June 2006.

These children are holding a memorial in remembrance of those who died in the 2004 tsunami. Even with the warning system, children in South Asia still face the threat of future disasters.

Warning systems save lives

Despite the new Indian Ocean warning system, there are still problems. Poor countries that surround the Indian Ocean have no way to warn people near coastlines. Most people still do not know what to do when told that a tsunami is coming, and in some places there is not enough money to spend on teaching them.

However, even a well-prepared country can be devastated by a tsunami. In March 2011, a huge tsunami swept across the coast of Japan. The country had a good warning system, and people were trained in what to do if a tsunami struck. Unfortunately, the tsunami happened very fast. There was not enough time for people to get to safety. Thousands of people died, and almost half a million lost their homes. Although there were terrible losses, without Japan's warning system, many more people could have died. No one can prevent a tsunami, but warning systems can save lives.

The Japan tsunami reached a height of 10 metres (33 feet) as it struck the coastal city of Sendai, sweeping cars away and destroying houses.

Mapping tsunamis

Tsunamis are a major threat to land near earthquake zones. However, as the Newfoundland disaster showed, tsunamis can strike at any seacoast.

Kelly's Cove, Newfoundland

In 1929, an earthquake caused a tsunami to sweep through Kelly's Cove in Newfoundland. Houses and buildings were destroyed.

Crescent City, California

The second-largest earthquake ever recorded struck Alaska in 1964. It caused tsunamis to sweep south and hit Crescent City. Eleven people there died.

Hilo, Hawaii

When a tsunami struck Hawaii in 1946, people fled to high ground for safety. A wave 42 metres (137 feet) high was recorded.

Kelly's Cove

NORTH AMERICA

Crescent City

ATLANTIC OCEAN

PACIFIC OCEAN

SOUTH AMERICA

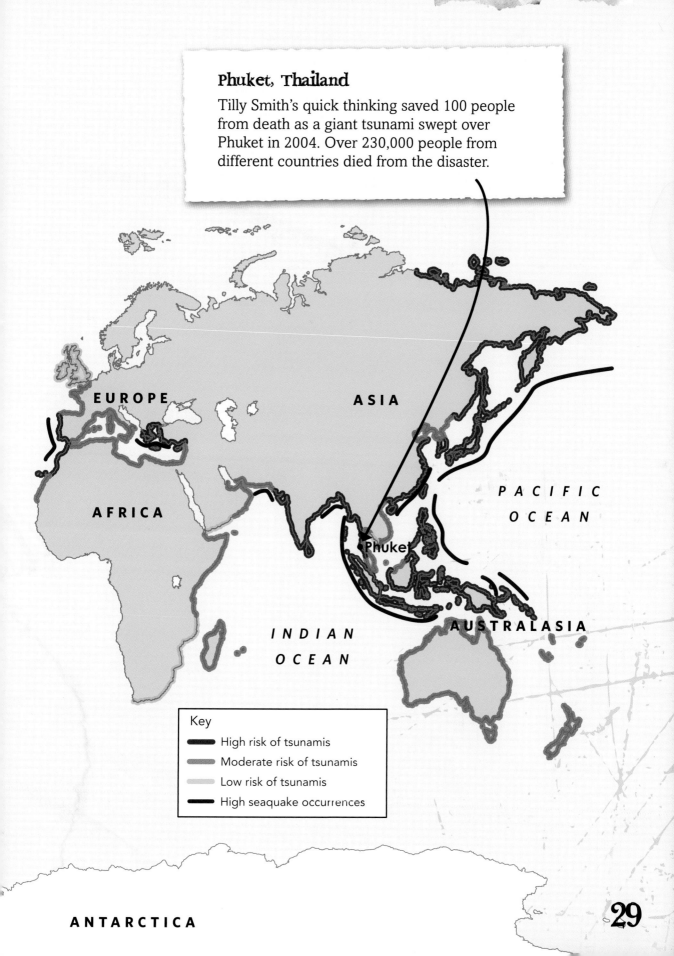

Phuket, Thailand

Tilly Smith's quick thinking saved 100 people from death as a giant tsunami swept over Phuket in 2004. Over 230,000 people from different countries died from the disaster.

EUROPE

ASIA

AFRICA

PACIFIC
OCEAN

Phuket

INDIAN
OCEAN

AUSTRALASIA

Key

High risk of tsunamis

Moderate risk of tsunamis

Low risk of tsunamis

High seaquake occurrences

ANTARCTICA

Glossary

Banda Aceh city on the northern tip of Sumatra, one of the islands of Indonesia

charity group group dedicated to helping people overcome problems, including disasters

currents part of a body of water moving in a certain direction

debris broken or ruined pieces of buildings, machines, or other objects

epicentre point on the ground just above where an earthquake starts and is strongest. A tsunami spreads out from the epicentre of an underwater earthquake.

inland area of land away from a coast or shore

lava solid black rock that forms when the liquid rock from a volcano cools

lighthouse building equipped with powerful lights to warn ships that the shoreline is near

machete long knife used for cutting down plants

monument structure or piece of art built as a reminder of an event or person

programme planner person who studies and puts together information for an organization

surge sudden movement of water

tremor shaking associated with an earthquake

United Nations organization made up of almost every country in the world. The organization works towards international peace, security, better living standards, and human rights.

Find Out More

Books

The Asian Tsunami 2004 (When Disaster Struck), John Townsend
(Raintree, 2006)

Earthquakes and Tsunamis (Amazing Planet Earth), Terry Jennings
(Franklin Watts, 2009)

Tsunamis and Floods (Graphic Natural Disasters), Gary Jeffery

(Franklin Watts, 2010)

On the Web

earthquakescanada.nrcan.gc.ca/histor/20th-eme/1929/1929-eng.php
Visit the National Resources Canada website to read an article on the
Newfoundland tsunami.

ioc3.unesco.org/itic/contents.php?id=332
Go to this website to download a cartoon booklet that gives advice for
children about what to do if a tsunami hits.

www.childrenoftsunami.info/heshani/bio.htm
Read Heshani Madushika Hewavitharana's story at the Children of
Tsunami's website.

www.nhm.ac.uk/nature-online/earth/volcanoes-earthquakes
Visit the Natural History Museum website to find out all about tsunamis
and other natural disasters.

www.npr.org/templates/story/story.php?storyId=5007860
This is a 2005 report by National Public Radio on the Crescent City tsunami
in California.

Index